MW01247303

The
TRUE COLORS
OF OUR
HEART

An Exploration of Sinful Feelings for Children

Barbara Bricker

ISBN 979-8-88943-743-7 (paperback)
ISBN 979-8-88943-744-4 (digital)

Copyright © 2023 by Barbara Bricker

All rights reserved. No part of this publication may be reproduced, distributed, or transmitted in any form or by any means, including photocopying, recording, or other electronic or mechanical methods without the prior written permission of the publisher. For permission requests, solicit the publisher via the address below.

Christian Faith Publishing
832 Park Avenue
Meadville, PA 16335
www.christianfaithpublishing.com

Printed in the United States of America

Introduction

I HAVE ALWAYS believed that it is important to acknowledge children's emotions. I believe it's crucial to their well-being to encourage them to talk about how they feel at certain times in their lives. This encouragement applies to not only "good" feelings, but to "bad" feelings as well.

Along with exploring feelings, I also wonder whether children actually grasp the concept of sin. Some seem to have a sense that sin is something bad, but I doubt that they realize how harmful sin is. Do they know that the "bad" feelings they sometimes have are actually results of sin? If left unaddressed, these sinful feelings can escalate to bad actions and, at the very least, will result in feeling worse.

As a Christian, I know that the Lord wants all his children to lead healthy and happy lives. He has provided an entire book filled with guidelines and protections so that we may all do just that. His book helps readers identify and explore feelings—both good and bad. It also gives helpful advice on how to deal with the bad feelings springing up as a result of sin.

For this study, I first considered tackling the "seven deadly sins." After research, however, I found several lists of sins throughout history. The list commonly referred to as the "seven deadly sins" is not found in the Bible but rather emerges from an original list of eight compiled by a fourth-century monk Evagrius Ponticus. John Cassian, a Christian monk and theologian (c. 360–435 AD), tweaked the list, and it eventually became part of Catholic devotions.

I also explored King Solomon's list found in the Old Testament in Proverbs 6:16–19 and the very extensive list found in the New Testament in Galatians 5:19–21. This last list was pretty compelling as it was followed by an equally extensive list of virtues also known to Christians as "fruit of the Holy Spirit."

The research of virtues sent me on a long journey into various philosophies and religions, including an interesting examination of the poem "Psychomachia" by Aurelius Clemens Prudentius from the fifth century AD. I quickly realized that if the varying opinions overwhelmed me, I would certainly lose the attention of my seven-to-ten-year-old reader. This meant addressing a smaller selection of sinful feelings and virtues or "cures" for this Bible study.

In the end, I chose to write about seven sinful feelings that I thought children might often experience. I liked the "Seven Deadly Sins" list, but due to the age of my reader, I decided to replace *lust* with *despair*.

When it came to the cures, as a Christian, I selected ones that should lead children to follow the New Commandment: to love God and to love their neighbor. Added to this rule is the reader's realization that by the main character "working the cure," he or she always enjoys a healthier, happier life.

It is my hope that Bible study teachers will explain that our king, Jesus, doesn't really turn our skin colors based on our sinful feelings. Ask the children how they would feel if their skin did change color, and explain that even though our skin doesn't change, Jesus still knows the condition of our hearts at all times.

My objectives for writing this book are as follows:

- to identify sinful feelings in a way children will understand;
- to help children see the importance of talking to Jesus about sinful feelings;
- to encourage children to follow his remedies for "curing" these feelings right away so that these feelings don't advance into sinful actions (the end result being that the children will be healthier and happier);

- to let them know that they can talk to the King anytime, anywhere;
- to help them see that Jesus does not condemn them but wants to help, walking alongside them to strengthen and guide them;
- to make sure they know that he loves them and always wants the best for them; and
- to provide children with ways to display the Commandment "Love God and love your neighbor."

I once heard a pastor say that in order to fully appreciate what Jesus did for us on the cross, we first have to recognize that we are sinners. Perhaps one of the greatest benefits of this study will be to introduce young children to the fact that they have sin in their lives—this being done in order for them to realize more quickly the gift of Jesus.

And even though "political correctness" is not high on my list of critical objectives, know that none of the selected feeling colors is meant to represent any ethnic group.

Scarlet Red = Anger

*Whoever is slow to anger has great understanding, but
he who has a hasty temper exacts folly.*

—Proverbs 14:29

Tim Purr Learns Patience

TIM PURR WAS fuming! Another soccer practice was over, and none of his teammates had passed him the ball—not even once. How was he ever going to kick a goal if he never got the ball? *That's it!* he thought as he trudged off toward the recreation center's locker room. He was going to talk to Dad about not playing anymore. In his fury, he kicked a teammate's water bottle off the nearest bench. The lid shot off, and the water flew everywhere.

"There's a kick for you!" he shouted.

In the locker room, Tim's bad **temper** continued to display itself. He slammed open locker doors as he made his way to his own locker. He was thinking about his last conversation with his father about playing soccer. Dad had gone on and on about learning to play on a team and the importance of practice. *Practice took too much time,* Tim thought. He just wanted to get the ball and make goals. He couldn't understand why his moron teammates didn't realize that.

When he had finished changing his clothes, he glared at his teammates as he passed by them on his way to the door. He didn't notice the wide-eyed stares he was receiving in return. Once in the hallway, he headed for the auto pickup queue to look for his dad's car. Spotting it, he quickly charged toward it, opened the back door, got in, slammed the car door shut harder than necessary, and buckled up. His dad, who had been staring at Tim in the rearview mirror, carefully drove the car out of the queue. Instead of heading home, however, Tim noticed that he drove over to the parking lot at the community park. "Hey, what's up?" Tim asked.

His dad said, "Practice didn't go well today, I see."

Tim just rolled his eyes and asked, "How could you tell?"

Mr. Purr turned the rearview mirror so that Tim could see himself. Tim's mouth dropped open when he saw his reflection. His skin had turned a dark scarlet red!

With a fearful voice, Tim asked, "Dad, what's wrong with my skin?"

His dad thought for a minute before speaking and then said, "Tim, I don't think your skin color is the problem. To find out what the real problem is, it would be best for you to have a good talk with the King of Children's Hearts."

He had Tim get out of the car, and he steered him toward the path into the park. "You'll find the King there," he said. Tim nodded and headed down the path. He soon saw the King sitting on a bench. The King smiled at Tim as he approached, gave him a high five, and asked him to sit by him.

The King said, "Tim, it looks like things haven't been going your way today. Why don't you tell me about it." Tim began telling him about his soccer teammates not passing the ball to him. The King asked him how this had made him feel.

"Mad as fire! And I made sure they all knew it too—the morons!" He briefly paused and then asked, "Is that why my skin is red?"

The King explained that sometimes, his children had to have his gentle, loving discipline in order to get better at showing their love for him and for others. When this was necessary, he allowed their skin to change color—showing the true color of their heart at that time. He said the scarlet red skin color meant that Tim was experiencing unjustified anger.

"Unjustified, what does that mean?" Tim asked.

The King said that Tim's teammates hadn't passed him the ball because they were trying to be mean to him but because they knew Tim wasn't ready to handle the ball properly. "This was probably due to the coach's instructions. So being angry with them wasn't justified—it wasn't right," he said. "Unjustified anger reveals a lack of love and is unhealthy for everyone involved," he added.

"Well, am I the only one who ever feels this way? And is my skin always going to be this color?" Tim asked worriedly.

The King shook his head and told Tim that he often saw this type of anger in his children and that there was a cure.

Tim looked up hopefully and asked, "What?"

The King said that for the next three days, he wanted Tim to take the time to understand the needs and desires of others before acting or speaking. "This is called patience, Tim. And patience cures unjustified anger by helping you stop and think about someone else's needs and motives before just reacting based on what you are feeling or thinking."

Tim thought for a minute and replied, "I think I can do that, King, if you will help me."

The King smiled and said, "I will always be with you, Tim."

When Tim arrived back at the car, he smiled at his dad and got in the car without slamming the door. On the way home, he thought about what the King had said. When they arrived home, Tim asked his dad if he would take him to the recreation center the next day. The coach had mentioned something about having an extra Saturday practice. His dad said that he would be happy to.

Later that night, Tim was building a tower with his wooden blocks. Suddenly, his little brother, Sammy, came over and crashed into it. The blocks tumbled everywhere. Tim's parents turned to see what had happened and held their breath, waiting for the explosion they felt sure would come. Tim jumped up, clenching and releasing his fists, and trying everything in his might to hold back the word "stupid" that he usually called his brother at times like this. Instead, he said under his breath, "Please help me, dear King." After a minute, he calmly sat down and asked his brother, "Why did you do that, Sammy?"

Sammy stared up at him and said, "'Cause I want you to play with me now."

Tim nodded his head and realized that he hadn't played with his brother for quite a while. He said, "Okay, why don't we build a fort with these blocks, but first, you'll have to help pick them up."

Their parents couldn't believe what they had just witnessed, but Mr. Purr smiled as he saw that Tim's skin had just turned from dark scarlet to watermelon red.

The next day, Tim was up early and ready for soccer practice. When he arrived at the soccer field, Tim had to endure a little ribbing from his teammates about his new skin color, but he took several deep breaths and remained calm. He soon realized that they weren't trying to pick on him but were just teasing him a little. Today, at practice, Tim was determined not to concentrate on getting the ball passed to him, but just on being a part of the team.

When practice was over, he decided to go over to the teammate whose water bottle he had kicked the day before. Tim told the boy, Colton, that he was sorry for having done that and offered him his own water bottle.

Colton, who Tim realized was one of the better players on the team, said, "No problem!"

As Tim started to walk away, Colton said, "You know you're getting a lot better at soccer."

"Really?" Tim asked.

"Yeah, but I think your passing skills still need some work. If you want, I could stay after practice and work with you on it," he offered. Tim said that that would be great and thanked him. Colton said, "Sure. We've all been where you are now. It just takes lots of practice, but I think you'll be a really great player before long."

Throughout the rest of the weekend, Tim continued to work on his feelings of anger. He played more with Sammy and realized that his little brother just loved him and liked being around him. He even showed patience on Sunday when that old lady at church, who wore a lot of perfume, grabbed him and hugged him like she did every Sunday. This time, instead of wincing and trying to wiggle free, he actually heard her as she explained that he reminded her a lot of her grandson who had moved far away with his parents. Tim could tell that she missed her grandson terribly and decided that a weekly hug from her might not be as bad as all that.

When his dad picked him up after school on Monday, he asked Tim if he might want to give the King of Children's Hearts an update. Tim readily agreed.

The King was sitting on the same park bench and was very glad when Tim came and sat by him. The King asked Tim to tell him what had been happening since their last long talk. Tim told him about his brother aggravating him, his soccer teammates laughing at him, and even about the old lady at church trying to hug him to death. The King laughed out loud when Tim got to that last part.

"What have you learned from all this?" the King asked.

Tim thought for a bit and said, "I've learned that instead of just immediately getting angry at everything, if I just wait a minute and take a deep breath, a lot of times, there's no reason to be angry at all." The King smiled and nodded. "Like with my brother, he just does things to get my attention sometimes because he misses playing with me. And you were right. My teammates weren't being mean to me. They knew I needed more practice. And that old lady at church is just missing her grandson, and I'm just a sort of substitute for him I guess. I learned that if I use patience, I'll be able to see what others are feeling and what makes them do the things they do. And I'll be able to show love to them instead of getting mad at them."

"You've learned a great deal, my child," the King said.

"But, dear King," Tim said, "I sure couldn't have done this without you. Thank you for being with me and helping me. I love you most of all." The King smiled, gave Tim a big high five, and watched as he raced back to the car, a slight pink flush on his skin.

Study Questions:

1. Why was Tim so angry?
2. Where did Tim talk with the King?
3. How did Tim feel when he showed patience to others?

Thinkin' Cap Questions:

1. In your life, are there times when you get angry?
2. Can you think of ways to show patience?

Find the mystery character word.

Blue = Despair

For you are my hope, Lord God, my security since I was young. I depend on you since birth, when you brought me from my mother's womb; I praise you continuously.

—Psalm 71:5–6

Missy Ree Finds Hope

MISSY REE COULD not stop crying! Her dad had cancelled their Saturday together again. Missy buried her head in her pillow as she thought about the number of times he had cancelled since he had taken this new job. "I guess Daddy's new job means more to him than I do!" she cried.

For the rest of the morning, Missy stayed in her room, lying face down on her bed, and thinking about how her life had gone from bad to worse. First, her grandmother, Nanna, had gotten sick and later died. She missed her so much. Then Daddy had taken a new job and was working a lot. The new job was in another town, so they had to move, which meant Missy had to change schools and leave all her friends.

At lunchtime, her mother came into Missy's room and gently patted her back. She told Missy that even though she understood that she was very sad, she still needed to eat something. Missy said, "Oh, why did Nanna have to die? She would have understood my **misery**! Daddy doesn't want to see me anymore, and now that we have moved, I'll never have any friends again…ever!" Missy's mother told her that things were going to be different for sure, but that there would be good times ahead. On hearing this, Missy rolled over and shouted, "No, I will never be happy again!"

Suddenly, Missy noticed the wide-eyed expression on her mother's face and asked, "Why are you looking at me like that, Mommy?"

Her mother picked up a mirror from the dresser and handed it to Missy. Staring back at Missy in the mirror was not her usual brown face but a blue one—tear-streaked and definitely navy blue!

"Oh, no! What has happened to my skin?"

Her mother told Missy that she thought it would be good if Missy had a nice talk with the King of Children's Hearts as he would be able to explain the skin change. She helped her daughter off the bed and led her to the back door. "Why don't you go sit in that swing on the back porch and wait for him there?"

Shortly, the King came walking into their backyard and up on the porch. He sat down by Missy and gave her a big hug. "I see that your lovely brown face has turned blue, my child. Tell me what has been happening lately."

The words just poured out of her as she told the King about her grandmother dying, her dad's new job, and their move, leaving all her friends behind.

"And now, my new problem is that my skin is blue!" she blubbered to a stop.

The King gave Missy another hug and said, "My dear child, sometimes, what seems like the problem is actually just a result of the real problem." The King explained that sometimes, his children had to have his gentle, loving discipline in order to get better at showing their love for him and for others. When this was necessary, he allowed their skin to change color—showing the true color of their heart at that time.

"Your face is blue right now because you have been experiencing the despair that comes from self-pity." Missy told the King that she was feeling very sad but didn't know that was wrong. The King explained that feeling sad at times in our lives was just a part of living in this world, but that we shouldn't let it get to the point that we felt everything was bad and was always going to be that way. "Self-pity means you are just looking at yourself and have taken your eyes off what is most important—loving me and loving others."

The King told Missy that sometimes, sadness is made worse by having unrealistic expectations of life in this world and not thinking ahead to how life will be in his heavenly kingdom. He told Missy that there was a way to change her skin back though. Missy quickly asked, "How?"

The King said that for the next three days, each time she felt self-pity, Missy must think of and focus on something positive, realistic, and hopeful. "Hope cures self-pity because it helps us to not focus on everything being perfect right now, but to look ahead to a wonderfully promised future."

Missy said that she wasn't really sure she could do that but would try. The King smiled and reminded Missy that he was always with her, especially when things were most difficult.

For the rest of the day, Missy thought about her talk with the King. The next day, she and her mother attended their new church. In her Sunday school class, they were talking about heaven. The teacher asked the class what they thought it would be like. It seemed like everyone had an opinion. Some involved clouds, others included wings and halos, and a boy named Joey sounded really sure that he was going to have a mansion that was on a street of gold.

The teacher then read something from the Bible about heaven. The scripture said that in heaven, there would be no more crying, sadness, pain, and death. She went on to talk about them living in heaven someday because of their friendship with the King. She said, "We will be able to see people again who have died. And how nice it will be to see them happy and healthy."

On the way home from church, Missy was thinking about how sick her grandmother had been before she died and how sad she had been since her death. But then those sad thoughts were replaced with a picture of Nanna laughing and walking without her legs hurting. She was glad that Nanna was in heaven. Missy knew that it wasn't very realistic to think that Nanna would live forever here on earth. She knew that she would still miss her sometimes, but she had the real hope that she would see her again. Missy suddenly felt very happy.

On Monday morning, Missy walked down to the school bus stop. She was feeling a bit anxious about riding the bus to her new school for the first time. The feeling was made worse by the fact that her face was still blue—maybe not navy blue, but more of a blueberry blue. Missy noticed a girl about her age waiting too. They exchanged half smiles. When the bus came, the girl got on and found a seat with another girl who looked like a good friend as they immediately began chatting. Missy found a seat further back and on the ride to school thought about her best friend, Ellyanna, back at her old school. She started feeling very sad, thinking that she probably would never find a really good friend again. She was trying very hard to feel hopeful and positive and quietly said, "Dear King, I need your help."

Just then, she noticed that someone sat in the seat right beside her. She turned and was surprised to see the girl from the bus stop sitting there. The girl said, "Hi, I'm Shiloh, and I live next door to you. Do you like jumping on the trampoline? I have one in my yard."

Missy said that she sure did like jumping. Shiloh said that maybe Missy could come over when they got home from school. Then she asked Missy who her teacher would be and found that they were in the very same class. Shiloh said that she would show Missy around and even introduce her to some of her friends. Missy told her "thank you" and thought that even though she would miss Ellyanna and her old friends, she felt happy to know that Shiloh lived right next door. She was hopeful that she would meet more new friends just as nice as she was.

When Missy got home from school, her mother asked how her day had gone. Missy told her about Shiloh, all the new kids she had met at school, and about being invited to jump on the trampoline. "You may go over and jump for about an hour as soon as your homework is done," her mother said.

Missy excitedly yelled, "Thanks, Mommy!" as she raced down the hall to her bedroom to start to work on her homework. Her mother was happy to see the sky blue color of her daughter's face.

Later that evening, as they ate dinner, Missy was busy telling her mother all about the fun she had at Shiloh's house. Her mother suggested that perhaps Shiloh could come with them the following weekend. "Your father wants to take us to the zoo," she said.

"Daddy will be home this weekend? He doesn't have to work out of town?" Missy asked.

Her mother explained that Daddy had been working out of town a good bit because he had been going through training for his new job. "But he's through with that now and should be home on weekends."

Missy was about to burst with happiness. After she had helped with the dishes, Missy asked if she could go sit on the back porch for a little while. Her mother smiled and nodded.

Before long, the King came and sat by her on the porch swing and asked how things had been going. Missy told him that things were much better than when they had last spoken. She told him about the things she learned about heaven, her new friend Shiloh, and about her father being finished with his job training.

The King said, "Wow, sounds like things are looking up in your life!"

Missy said that they sure were. "And you know, it's funny what you said about looking up because I think that's why things are better…because I'm looking up and… ahead! I've learned that things won't always go as I expect them to, but that doesn't mean everything is bad." The King was nodding as Missy went on. "Like my thinking the worst about Daddy when in my heart, I knew that he was doing what he had to do. Instead of getting sad and mad at him, I should have shown him more love because I knew that he loves me and Mommy lots and lots. And even though I was sad that I would miss my old friends, I knew that they weren't the only friends in the whole wide world." The King smiled.

"But, dear King, I was the happiest when I was learning more about heaven and thinking about seeing Nanna again. I wouldn't be able to do that unless you had done what you did for us. You are the biggest reason I am hopeful about good things happening!" The King gave Missy a big hug and told her that he was so pleased to see that her warm brown skin wasn't blue anymore.

As he rose to leave, he said, "Remember Missy, in the future, when you start to feel self-pity, think it through and always…look up!"

Study Questions:

1. Do we have to be happy all the time?
2. Who is the King of Children's Hearts?
3. Did the King help Missy?

Thinkin' Cap Questions:

1. How is self-pity different than just being sad sometimes?
2. Why is the King our hope?

Find the mystery character word.

Green = Envy

A heart at peace gives life to the body, but envy rots the bones.

—Proverbs 14:30

Gell Luss Shows Kindness

GELL COULDN'T BELIEVE her eyes! The new girl, Cindy, or "Little Miss Has It All" as Gell secretly called her, stood in class, showing off the new jeweled headband placed on her perfectly straight blonde hair. It matched her expensive outfit too—right down to her darling, little purple shiny shoes.

Gell stormed out of the classroom and into the bathroom to escape the scene. She marched back and forth, periodically running a hand through her curly-to-the-point-of-being-frizzy flaming red hair. As she paced, she remembered how she had seen that very same headband in a store at the mall. She had asked her mother if she could have it. Mom had given her usual answer, which included a long speech about how the Luss family was being careful with money right now and needed to focus on items they needed, not on ones they just wanted. In other words…no!

Gell stopped pacing to glance in the mirror over the sink and let out a yell. What in the world? Her skin had turned a deep emerald green! Gell raced out of the bathroom and down the hall to the school nurse's office. She ran through the door and right into Nurse Dixon. Gell said, "Look at my face! It's *green*!"

Nurse Dixon told Gell to sit down and calmly tell her what had happened right before Gell noticed her new skin color. Gell explained about the headband while Nurse Dixon listened, nodding her head every now and then. When Gell finished, Nurse Dixon said that this seemed like a problem that would take more than her medical skills to fix. She advised Gell to have a visit with the King of Children's Hearts and to do so as quickly as possible.

Gell was ushered into a quiet office where she could have an undisturbed visit with the King. He gave her a warm hug, asked her to sit by him and to tell him about her problem. "My problem? My problem is that my skin is green!" she said.

He gave a slight smile and said, "My dear child, sometimes, what seems like the problem is actually just a result of the real problem." The King explained that sometimes, his children had to have his gentle, loving discipline so they could get better at showing their love for him and for others. When this was necessary, he allowed their skin to change color—showing the true color of their heart at that time.

Gell looked a bit confused, so the King went on to explain that the green color of her skin meant that she was experiencing something called envy.

Gell asked, "What is envy, and how can I fix it?"

The King said that envy means being jealous of another's possessions, looks, and abilities. "You wanted what Cindy had, and you didn't want her to have it either. Envy reveals a lack of love and is unhealthy for everyone involved."

The King patted Gell on the shoulder and said that all his children, at one time or another, experienced envy. He said that there was a way to cure her skin.

Gell quickly looked up at him and asked, "How?"

The King said that for the next three days, Gell must show kindness to others even if they seemed to have everything—or at least everything that Gell wanted for herself. He said that looking for ways to be kind to others and being thankful for what we have can result in a peaceful heart.

Gell asked, "That's it? I need to show kindness to others to turn my skin back to its regular color?"

The King said, "Yes, Gell, as kindness cures envy by placing your desire to help others above your need to have more than they have."

Gell nodded her head and assured the King that she would sure try. The King smiled and said, "Good. And, remember, I will be with you every step of the way."

Gell was happy to finally get home after enduring stares and smirks from the kids on the school bus. She was glad that the next day was Saturday! At home, her mother took one look at Gell and gave her a big hug. After dinner, her mom told Gell that she wanted her to come with her on an errand in the morning. Gell opened her mouth to complain that Saturday was cartoon day on TV, but she stopped herself because suddenly, she had this feeling that that wouldn't be a kind thing to do. So in a nice way and without complaining, Gell agreed to go.

The next day, Gell and her mother headed out to take some old clothes to a homeless shelter. On the way, her mother stopped at a convenience store to let Gell pick out something from the candy aisle as a treat for herself. She selected three of her favorite suckers. When they arrived at the shelter, Gell saw some children sitting at a table. Their clothes were old and didn't fit very well. Each of them had a bowl of cereal before them, and they were eating like they hadn't eaten in days.

Gell sneered at them and said to her mother, "Wow, they sure look like they love Flakes 'n' Loops!" Her mother explained that that was probably the only meal they would have for the entire day. She told Gell that they did not have a home because their parents were going through a very hard time. She said that the people at the shelter had told her that the family had slept in their car the night before.

Gell's face dropped. She felt sad and ashamed for making fun of them. Suddenly, she knew what she wanted to do. She went over and pulled the three suckers out of her pocket. She placed them on the table and smiled at the children. Gell's mother, who was watching the scene, just smiled and nodded her head. Gell didn't notice, but her skin had just changed from a dark emerald green to more of a pickle green color.

On Sunday, Gell and her family attended church. When she went into her Sunday school class, she noticed that Cindy from school was in the class too. She was sitting by herself, and she was wearing that headband.

Oh, great, I have to see her at school and now church too! Gell thought. But then she overheard two teachers talking about Cindy. They said how sad it was that Cindy's parents had been killed in a car accident earlier in the year. Cindy was living with a childless uncle who thought that just buying her a lot of stuff might make her happy.

Gell thought about how sad she would feel if she didn't have her parents and immediately felt sorry that she had been **jealous** of Cindy. She decided to go over and sit by her and even introduce her to some of the kids in the class.

By Monday morning, Gell's skin had turned a lighter celery color, which made returning to school almost bearable. Throughout the day, Gell continued to look for ways to show kindness. At the end of the day, she decided to go and visit the King of Children's Hearts.

He was very glad to see Gell. After a hug, she sat down by him. The King asked Gell how the last three days had been for her. She shared her experiences with the King. She told him about treating her mom with more kindness and respect, about the kids at the homeless shelter, and even about Cindy being in her Sunday school class. The King was smiling and nodding as she relayed her stories.

When she stopped to take a breath, the King asked, "What have you learned from these experiences?"

Gell pursed her lips and twirled a strand of her unruly hair as she thought about the past three days. "I've learned that I should like the way things are in my life—my parents, my home, and my clothes. And not to be **jealous** of people like Cindy because even though it looks like things are better for them, you never know what they are going through. I'm happier. I even like my wild red hair more!" The King smiled.

"And there's something else, dear King," Gell said.

The King's eyebrows raised as he asked, "Really, what is that, my child?"

Gell smiled up at him and said, "I feel love and thankfulness to you for disciplining me because I know you did it out of love for me."

Gell noticed that the King's eyes glistened as he smiled down at her, and she thought she saw a tear in his eye.

He gave her another hug and said, "That is what I wanted you to learn, dear child."

Gell thanked the King again and headed for the door.

"Oh, and, Gell, there's one more thing."

"What is that?" Gell asked as she turned back toward the King.

"I just love your wild red hair! It is a special part of you, and it looks so pretty with your peachy pink skin!"

Gell beamed as she left the room and raced to catch the school bus.

Study Questions:

1. Why was Gell so upset about Cindy?
2. Was the King angry with Gell because of her sinful feeling?
3. How did showing kindness make Gell feel?

Thinkin' Cap Questions:

1. In your life, are there times when you feel envious?
2. Can you think of ways to show kindness to people?

Find the mystery character word (2 times).

Orange = Gluttony

For whether you eat or drink or whatever you do, do it all for the glory of God.

—1 Corinthians 10:31

Cray Vinn Learns Self-Control

CRAY WAS FEELING sick. He thought to himself, *Maybe I shouldn't have had that last chocolate cookie; but those cookies were so good, especially with that creamy icing on top.* He felt stuffed and miserable. There was no way he was going to be able to join in the camp activities now. If he participated in the sack jump, rope pull, or even the egg roll, he might just "toss his cookies"…literally!

Cray collapsed in a hammock, patting his expanded belly. He watched as his best friend from church, Jimmy, walked by with a group of other boys. Jimmy had been spending less time with Cray lately, even to the point of ignoring him. He thought about Jimmy's hurtful words yesterday when he told Cray that it wasn't any fun to be his friend anymore. Jimmy said that all Cray wanted to do was lay around eating and watching TV. He said that Cray was always too full to do any of the fun stuff that was available to them here at camp.

Cray turned away from the scene while contemplating Jimmy's words. He felt a shadow fall over him and heard Camp Counselor Steve ask, "Cray Vinn, are you just going to swing in that hammock all week? Feeling too full again today to enjoy the activities with the other boys?"

As Cray turned toward him, he noticed the sudden wide-eyed expression on Counselor Steve's face. Alarmed, Cray asked, "What's wrong?"

Counselor Steve motioned for Cray to follow him. He led him to the old but shiny meal gong hanging from the porch rafters of the Cafeteria Hall. "Look at yourself, Cray!" he said.

As Cray stared at his reflection, his expression mirrored Counselor Steve's wide-eyed one earlier. "Oh, no, why is my skin dark orange? What's going on?"

Counselor Steve patted Cray on the back and said that instead of receiving counsel from him, it might be best if Cray had a direct talk with the King of Children's Hearts. He advised Cray to take a walk in the prayer circle and look for the King there.

Cray headed off quickly to the prayer circle to look for the King. He found him sitting on an old log at the center of the circle. As Cray approached, the King looked up, smiled, and asked him how camp was going. Cray started to say, "Just fine until my skin turned orange," but then thought that that wasn't quite true.

Instead, he told the King about Jimmy not wanting to be friends with him because he just wanted to eat and watch TV. "And, on top of that, my new problem is that my skin has turned orange!" Cray finished.

The King nodded and said, "My dear child, sometimes, what seems like the problem is actually just a result of the real problem." The King explained that sometimes, his children had to have his gentle, loving discipline in order to get better at showing their love for him and for others. When this was necessary, he allowed their skin to change color—showing the true color of their heart at that time.

The King went on to explain that the orange color of Cray's skin was a result of something called gluttony. He continued by telling Cray that gluttony is an unnatural excessive appetite or **craving**. "Things like eating or drinking too much are examples. But so are things like watching too much TV and playing too many video games. Sometimes, gluttony includes demanding too much from other people, like their time and attention," the King explained. "Doing anything to excess and not knowing when enough is enough is unhealthy and results in a less than happy life."

He then told Cray that there was a way to cure gluttony and return his skin to its natural color. Cray looked at the King hopefully and asked, "How?"

The King said that for the next three days, Cray must use self-control, which means stopping himself when he reached the "enough" point. He said that looking for ways to be content with less would mean that Cray would have a healthier body and better relationships. "It takes practice but will soon help you take the focus off yourself and turn it toward loving me and others."

The King noticed that Cray was seriously thinking about all he had said. He smiled and reminded Cray that he would be successful if he relied on the King's strength throughout the process.

Cray left the prayer circle and walked back toward the camp, thinking about the King's words. Instead of heading toward the hammock, he decided to go check out how his fellow campers were doing in the games. He still felt too full to participate in them, but he decided that he could at least cheer them on. It felt good to be out in the sunshine and be a part of the activities, even with his orange face. Jimmy saw him and gave him a slight nod of recognition.

Later that night, Cray decided to eat a sandwich for dinner and tried very hard to pass by the desserts. He ended up grabbing a cookie…but only one…and set down at the checkers table instead of going into the TV room. Before long, a boy came and sat opposite him, and they enjoyed several good games before "lights out" was called and each headed to their respective cabins. If Cray had glanced in the shiny meal gong, he would have been pleased to see that his skin had turned a lighter pumpkin orange color.

The next morning, Cray dressed in his bathing suit and a T-shirt and headed to the Cafeteria Hall for breakfast. His usual practice was to get there ahead of everyone so that he could have first shot at the bacon and lots of it. Today, he arrived later and only took a couple of slices of bacon to join the scrambled eggs on his plate. After breakfast, he headed to the roped-off swimming portion of the lake. He peeled off his T-shirt, ran down the dock, and jumped into the cool water. Before long, he was joined by other boys, all splashing each other and seeing how high they could jump on the big, bouncy water float. Cray thought how much more fun this was than sitting in front of the TV all day. He noticed a little later that Jimmy arrived and joined in the fun. When Cray managed to do a particularly high jump, which resulted in a huge splash, Jimmy gave him a fist bump.

Later that night, the campers set around the fire, listening to the camp counselors tell funny jokes and share interesting camp stories. At dinner, Cray had to ask the King to give him his strength to pass up on dessert but was glad that he had so that he could now enjoy roasting a few marshmallows over the fire with the other kids.

Cray again practiced self-control the next day at breakfast and joined Jimmy at the table with only a bowl of cereal and an orange. They made plans to meet at the rope walk as soon as Cray finished an errand. He wanted to go find the King of Children's Hearts for a little talk.

The King was sitting on the same log in the middle of the prayer circle and was very glad to see Cray. The King asked how things had been going. Cray told him about eating less—even passing up on desserts—and how that had resulted in him not only feeling a lot better, but also having more fun. The King was smiling and nodding as Cray talked.

"Sometimes, it was really hard not to eat more, and I want to thank you, dear King, for giving me your strength during those times," Cray said.

The King smiled and told Cray that he would always be with him to help strengthen him. The King asked Cray what he had learned from the experience. Cray thought about the past few days and told the King that he learned that using self-control wasn't always easy, but it was worth it. That he felt better, not stuffed and sickly. "And feeling better allowed me to do more fun stuff," Cray said. "I felt happier, especially when my friend Jimmy wanted to hang around me again." He told the King that he realized he hadn't been a very good friend to Jimmy and had let him down by letting his overeating and nonstop TV watching get in the way of their friendship.

"Most of all, dear King, I learned that you love me and want me to have a happy life. And that you give me the strength I need to get through the hard stuff in life." Cray finished.

The King nodded with a smile on his face, gave Cray a fist bump, and said, "Thank you for giving me an update. I love when my children want to talk to me, not just when needing my strength, but to thank me for the help given. Now, you'd better go meet Jimmy and remember to put some sunscreen on so you don't burn your fair skin!"

Study Questions:

1. Is it wrong to like to eat?
2. Why did the counselor want Cray out of the hammock?
3. How did Cray let his friend Jimmy down?

Thinkin' Cap Questions:

1. Do you have an unhealthy appetite for things?
2. What can you do to correct the problem?

Find the mystery character word.

Gold = Greed

Keep your lives free from the love of money and be content with what you have, because God has said, "Never will I leave you; never will I forsake you."

—Hebrews 13:5

Ava Rice Becomes Generous

"THAT'S MINE!" AVA Rice yelled as she snatched the doll from her friend Ellis's hands.

"I was only playing with it," Ellis replied, with a hurt look in her eyes. Ava didn't understand why her friend couldn't appreciate that she didn't like others holding her dolls. She liked them to stay lined up on the window seat in her room so she could look at all the different ones she had. So many, in fact, that Ava realized she would soon have to find another place to put any new ones as the window seat was full. Anyway, she wondered, why didn't Ellis play with her own dolls and bring one or two with her when she came to Ava's house to play?

Ava's parents were somewhat overly generous to their only child by providing her with new dolls on almost any occasion. Ava knew that Ellis wasn't an only child but rather one of five children in her family. Maybe that meant Ellis couldn't have a new doll whenever she wanted one, but surely, she had dolls that her older sisters could hand down to her or something.

Regardless, Ava thought, *I do not want to share any of my pretty dolls with anyone. I want them all to myself.*

As Ava arranged the snatched doll back in her position on the window seat, she noticed a strange golden reflection on the window glass. She peered in closer to see what it was and realized that it was coming from her face. Her face was a very shiny gold color! She whirled around and caught the open-mouthed, shocked expression on Ellis's face.

"What is wrong with your skin?" Ellis asked. "Why is it gold-colored?"

Ava said in a frightened voice, "I don't know!"

Ellis thought for a moment and said that one time, her older sister Jan's skin had turned gold when it was discovered that she had taken all the chocolate drops out of the candy jar and had hidden them in her bedroom so none of her sisters or brothers could have any.

"What happened?" Ava asked. "How did she get her skin to turn back to its regular color?" Ellis explained that her mother advised her sister to have a visit with the King of Children's Hearts so he could explain. She did, and the King helped her get back to normal.

Ava said that was what she would do—and fast! She ran into the den where the family met each week for home Bible study and found the King waiting for her. He took one look at Ava's face, gave her a quick hug, and invited her to tell him why she had come to see him.

"Why? Well, because my skin is shiny gold!" she answered.

He gave a slight smile and said, "My dear child, sometimes, what seems like the problem is actually just a result of the real problem." The King explained that sometimes, his children had to have his gentle, loving discipline in order to get better at showing their love for him and for others. When this was necessary, he allowed their skin to change color—showing the true color of their heart at that time.

The King said that the gold color of her skin meant that she was experiencing something called greed.

Ava looked uncomfortable, squirming a bit in her seat, and said, "So it's like this because I'm greedy?"

The King said that greed showed a lack of consideration for others. "You like to keep an overabundance of things for yourself when it might be better to give them away, especially if it helps others. Greed or **avarice** reveals a lack of love and is unhealthy for everyone involved."

The King told Ava that all his children, at one time or another, acted greedily. Ava nodded her head and said, "Dear King, Ellis said that her sister had this happen and that you were able to help her skin get back to its regular color. Can you help me?"

The King nodded and said that for the next three days, Ava must show generosity—learning to be content with less herself and more charitable or giving to others. He said that looking for ways to be less stingy and to stop trying to have more than everyone else would be a good start. "Sometimes, this includes more than just having more things than others. It can also mean that if you are better at something than others, don't use those skills and talents to take advantage of them to benefit yourself."

Ava nodded and said, "I think I understand, but I know I am going to need your help to change."

The King said, "I will help you as you learn to be generous, putting the desire to help others above storing up treasures for yourself."

On Monday morning, Ava was anxious to get to class as it was spelling bee day and she was the best speller in her class. Her teacher, Miss Simmons, always gave out stars to the winner, and Ava had the biggest collection of stars in class. The next best speller was Zane, but Ava noticed that lately, he didn't try all that much in the spelling contest and wondered if it was because she always seemed to win the stars. She felt a little bad about it as Zane was a nice boy and seemed to try really hard.

Ava decided to hold back just a little from jumping up and starting to spell each time Miss Simmons called out a word. Gradually, Zane began to stand up and start to spell. And Ava noticed other students start to do the same. She took her turn, too, but not enough to win the contest that day. But she thought, *How many stars did she really need any way?*

Saturday was going to be a great day as Ava planned to attend the County Fair with her parents. She was especially excited about the throwing-rings-around-the-pins game as she was an excellent thrower and was sure to win all the stuffed animal prizes. Ava gave her tickets to the man at the game and received her rings. She immediately started winning prizes and happened to notice two little children eyeing them. Ava realized that they were much too small to be very good at this game and would probably never win any prizes themselves. She thought, *Too bad for them*. But then she remembered what the King had said about generosity. She knew that she had a toy chest at home full of stuffed animals, so she turned toward the children and gave them the stuffed animals she had won. They squealed with delight! Ava was surprised at how good it felt to have made their day. Her parents, standing nearby, looked at each other in surprise but were glad to see Ava's actions, and her face became less shiny.

After church on Sunday, Ellis came over to Ava's house to play. Instead of forbidding her friend to touch her dolls, Ava shocked Ellis by not only inviting her to pick out her favorite doll and ones for her sisters, but also gave the dolls to them as gifts. Ellis immediately ran to Ava and hugged her and told her that she was the very best friend in the whole wide world. Ava realized that she had plenty of dolls and what good did it do to just have them sitting around, and it sure felt good to make her friend so happy.

On Sunday evening, Ava's skin had turned a much less shiny gold color, and she decided to go and update the King of Children's Hearts.

The King immediately noticed Ava's less bright skin color and asked her to tell him how the last three days had been for her. She told him about holding back a bit and letting Zane win the spelling bee stars and how happy he looked. She also told him about going to the fair and not feeling like she had to win all the throwing game prizes and how she actually gave the ones she had won to a couple of little kids. Then she told him about letting Ellis pick out her favorite doll and also the ones for her sisters and giving them to them. "It was kinda hard to do, but it sure did feel good to see how happy everyone was!" Ava explained.

"And there's something else, dear King," Ava said.

The King's eyebrows raised as he asked, "What, my child?"

Ava told him that in children's church that morning, they talked about the King's gift to everyone. "And I realized that you showed more generosity than anyone else as you gave yourself to us all."

The King smiled and nodded at Ava. He gave her a hug and said, "That is a very important thing to learn, my child." Ava smiled happily at him.

"And, Ava, even though your heart isn't shiny gold anymore, it is more precious to me than real gold."

Study Questions:

1. Was Ava mean to her friend?
2. Is it okay to have a lot of toys?
3. Is it okay to be really good at something?

Thinkin' Cap Questions:

1. How did being generous feel to Ava?
2. How was the King the most generous?

Find the mystery character word.

Gray = Laziness

Go to the ant, you sluggard; consider its ways and be wise.

—Proverbs 6:6

Idele Ness Learns Diligence

IDELE NESS WATCHED as the Youth Choir Director singled Annabelle Taylor out to sing the solo in the Church Musical…again! And while she agreed that Annabelle did have a really pretty voice, Idele sometimes wondered why she even bothered with all these choir practices. Her voice was just okay at best, and she didn't feel like it would be missed if she wasn't there. How much better it would be to just be at home this Friday afternoon, playing a video game or watching *Kids Club* on TV.

As the choir practice progressed, she sang the words to "This Little Light of Mine" with less and less enthusiasm—even the fun "stomp my feet, clap my hands, shout!" part that she liked best. She didn't notice the confusion and worry on the face of her friend, Mary, who stood beside her, nor did she notice the looks of concern from the director, Miss Rockwell.

51

When practice was over, the children started to carefully exit the choir ramps. With a bored expression, Idele made her way toward the door. Miss Rockwell met her there and asked to have a little chat. She said that she noticed Idele hadn't sung with her usual enthusiasm and asked what the problem was. Idele said that she felt she really didn't have much to contribute to the choir anymore.

She said, "I'm bored with it!"

Miss Rockwell said, "Well, I can take one look at your face and tell that."

Idele looked up questioningly and asked, "You can?"

Miss Rockwell took a little compact mirror out of her purse, handed it to Idele, and said, "Here…see for yourself."

Idele looked at her face in the mirror and couldn't believe that her face had turned a very dull gray color! "What's up?" Idele exclaimed.

Miss Rockwell gave Idele a shoulder hug and said that the King of Children's Hearts would be able to explain. "I believe you will find him in my office."

Idele went into the little office right off the music room, where she could have a visit with the King. He gave her a big smile, asked her to sit by him, and tell him how things were going.

"Well, not too well evidently as my skin has turned this ugly gray! Miss Rockwell said that you could tell me why. Is it because of something I ate?" she asked.

He said, "My dear child, the skin color change isn't because of what you have eaten, but it is a result of something you have been feeling. The skin change isn't the real problem but is actually a result of the real problem." The King explained that sometimes, his children had to have his gentle, loving discipline in order to get better at showing their love for him and for others. When this was necessary, he allowed their skin to change color—showing the true color of their heart at that time.

Idele asked, "So my heart is this gray color?"

The King explained that the color of her skin meant that she was experiencing something called **idleness** or sloth. Idele looked a bit confused, so the King went on and said that this meant being bored, lazy, and uninterested in using one's talents and gifts to help others. Idele agreed that was how she had been feeling lately by wanting to give up on choir practice and just stay home, watch TV, or play video games.

The King gave Idele an understanding nod and said that all his children, at one time or another, allowed themselves to become idle. He said that there was a way to cure her skin though.

Idele quickly asked, "How?"

The King said that for the next three days, Idele must show diligence and zeal toward helping others.

Idele asked, "By doing that, my skin will turn back to its regular color?"

The King said, "Yes, Idele, as diligence, steadily working by using one's talents and skills, cures idleness by placing the interests of others above your desire to take the easy way out of life."

Idele nodded her head and told the King that she would look for ways to do this. The King smiled and said, "I will help you along the way."

When Idele arrived home, her brother Rhett met her at the door and asked if she would help him with memorizing his Bible verses. He said, "Please help me as you are so good at memorizing, and I want to learn how."

At first, she wanted to say "no" as she had just gotten home from choir practice and just wanted to collapse in front of the TV; but then she thought about the King saying that his children should use their skills and talents to help others. She said, "Sure, Rhett. Go get your assignment, and I'll help you." After an hour of working with her brother, Idele was a bit more tired but so happy to see her brother make real progress with his scriptures.

On Saturday morning, Idele noticed that her mother was baking cookies to take to the nursing home for the elderly shut-ins from their church. She asked Idele if she would mind helping her decorate them with Valentine hearts for the upcoming holiday. She said, "Idele, you just seem to have a flair for cookie decorating, and I know that the hearts will bring real smiles to the residents' faces."

Even though Idele wanted to play the new video game that her grandparents had sent her, she decided to put her talents to good use and help her mother. Later that day, when she went with her mother to deliver the cookies, she was filled with joy as she handed out the heart-laden, decorated cookies. She realized that these might be the only Valentine's Day gift these older people would receive, and she was so happy to be a part of making them feel loved.

By Sunday morning, Idele's skin had turned a mix of lighter gray and pink, which made it easier to line up in the choir for the Church Musical. Her friend, Mary, said that she was so happy to see Idele as she had been afraid that she would stop coming to choir.

She said, "Idele, you always sing the songs just right and with such enthusiasm that it encourages me to stay on key and to sing louder too. I sure am glad you're here."

Idele had no idea that Mary depended on her like that, and the thought made her sing all the songs with a light and happy heart. And when they got to the "This Little Light of Mine" song, Idele's foot stompin', hand clappin', and shout were the loudest in the whole choir. Idele noticed Miss Rockwell look up and smile at her several times during the concert.

At the end of the service, Idele asked her parents if it would be okay if she went to find the King of Children's Hearts. They said that that would be just fine and they would wait for her at the entrance to the car park.

The King was very glad to see Idele. He met her with a big smile and a hug and wanted to know all that had been happening since their last visit. She shared her experiences with the King. She told him about helping her brother with his Bible verses, decorating her mom's cookies with little hearts, and later helping to deliver those cookies to the nursing home. The King smiled and nodded as she relayed her stories. Then she told him about how Mary had told her that her voice and way of singing helped her friend a lot in choir.

When she finished, the King asked, "What have you learned from these experiences?"

Idele told him, "I've learned that I have been given talents and skills that I didn't even realize I had. And how others around me rely on me to use those, and that they are a real help to others." The King nodded his head.

"And," she continued, "even though it is easier to say no to opportunities to use my talents and skills and spend that time watching TV or playing a game, there's a lot more happiness in doing the opposite. It doesn't seem like work at all when you see how happy it makes others." The King smiled.

"And, dear King," Idele said. "Thank you for giving me these gifts and for providing me ways that I can use them to show my love for you and for others."

The King told her that she was very welcome and what a joy it was for him when his children came to realize and appreciate what Idele had. He said, "Idele, your skin is no longer that dull gray color. Now you can go out in the world and really let your little light shine!"

Study Questions:

1. Is it wrong to watch TV or play video games?
2. How can using our talents and skills help others?
3. Did the King understand Idele's problem?

Thinkin' Cap Questions:

1. Are there times when you feel like just giving up?
2. What things can you get busy doing to serve the King?

Find the mystery character word.

Purple = Pride

Instead of being motivated by selfish ambition or vanity, each of you should, in humility, be moved to treat one another as more important than yourself. Each should be concerned not only about your own interest, but about the interests of others as well.

—Philippians 2:3–4

Ego Trip Learns Humility

"THAT'S A STUPID idea!" **Ego Trip** exclaimed loudly—so loudly that several of the children in his youth group jumped.

Pastor Jay said, "Ego, first of all, we don't use that word in youth group, and, secondly, we need to hear each other's ideas completely before we—"

Before he could even finish his sentence, Ego interrupted by rolling his eyes and saying, "Before we make a decision. I know, I know. But why waste everyone's time? Matt always has stu…urr…bad ideas. Why don't we just use my idea for the Youth Fun Festival Game? It's the best."

Pastor Jay explained that while Ego's idea did have some merit, it was important to listen to the ideas from all who wanted to share. Ego rolled his eyes, slumped down in his chair, and looked bored as others shared some of their thoughts with the group.

While Nora Farley was explaining that she thought a dunking game with Pastor Jay as the target would be sure to raise money and be lots of fun, too, Ego stood up and chanted, "Dumb, dumb, dumb idea!" Nora immediately stopped talking and hung her head so others couldn't see how embarrassed she was.

Pastor Jay calmly looked at Ego but firmly explained that listening to others' ideas and using the best part of each would result in a better festival game. He went on to say that when people contributed ideas to an event, they were much more enthusiastic about working for its success.

Ego barely waited for him to finish before saying, "Well, if they would just use my idea and do what I tell them to do, the game would be plenty successful as I—" Ego stopped talking as he saw the looks of amazement on the faces of Pastor Jay and the others. "What? Why are you all looking at me like that?"

Pastor Jay asked Ego to come with him. Ego quickly followed him into the hall, where Pastor Jay explained that this might be a good time for Ego to have a visit with the King of Children's Hearts. "You'll find him in the youth study hall."

Ego rolled his eyes again as he turned and walked slowly toward the study hall. He took a quick glance in the hall mirror as he passed and stopped, not believing his eyes. His face was dark purple! Ego ran the rest of the way and right into the arms of the King. "Look at my skin color!" he exclaimed.

The King patted his back, sat him in a chair beside him, and explained that sometimes, his children had to have his gentle, loving discipline in order to get better at showing their love for him and for others. When this was necessary, he allowed their skin to change color—showing the true color of their heart at that time.

"Why is my heart purple?" Ego worriedly asked.

The King went on to explain that purple meant that Ego's heart was full of pride.

Ego asked, "Well, is that a bad thing? Shouldn't we be proud of stuff?"

The King said that feeling some pleasure or satisfaction about our achievements, qualities, or possessions wasn't in itself bad, but when that becomes an exaggerated view of oneself—usually achieved by putting others down—it is bad. "It can be very harmful to all involved."

The King said that all his children, at one time or another, experienced this type of pride and that it was often the root of so many bad things in their lives. He then told Ego that there was a way to cure his skin color.

"How?" Ego asked.

The King said that for the next three days, Ego must practice humility. He said that Ego must look for ways to put himself—his ideas and desires for recognition and control—last. And that he must really listen to others, looking for good qualities in them and for ways to build them up, encourage them, and serve them.

"You see, humility cures pride by taking our 'selves' out of the way and putting the focus on the needs of others and their need for the King."

Ego told the King that this sounded pretty hard to do. The King nodded and said, "Yes, Ego, this is one of the most difficult tasks for my children, and because it is, I will be helping you along the way."

Later at home, Ego's mother asked him and his sister, Amy, to set the table for dinner. Usually, Ego got up, charged into the kitchen, collected all the dinnerware, utensils, and napkins, and set the table himself. He was always so annoyed when his little sister put napkins or forks at the wrong places and took forever doing it. She was slow and got things wrong, something he reminded her of each time. This time, however, he stopped and thought about what the King said about taking our "self" out of the way and focusing on others.

He turned to his sister and asked, "Amy, what is your favorite thing to do when we set the table for Mom?"

Amy told him that she liked putting the forks beside the plates as they were easier for her to handle.

He said, "Okay, then do you think it would be a good idea if I put out the plates and napkins, then you come right behind me and put the forks down?"

Amy smiled and said, "Yes, that sounds like a great idea!"

They worked together as a team and were finished in no time. When their mother complimented their work, Ego thought about taking all the credit, but instead, he said, "Thanks, Mom! And didn't Amy do a great job with the forks?" He really liked seeing the smile on his sister's face when she was included in the praise, and his mother enjoyed seeing Ego's face turn a lighter shade of purple.

The next day in class, the teacher called on Sammy Stevens to share his book report. Ego immediately rolled his eyes and thought, *Oh, no! There goes the rest of the class time.*

Sammy was such a slow reader. Usually, Ego said critical things to him or talked over him, sharing his own comments about the book. But this time, when he opened his mouth to speak, it was like he heard the King say, "Be still, my child. Learn more about Sammy, and look for ways to encourage, not criticize."

Ego remained silent, and at the end of class, he decided to go to the teacher and ask why Sammy read so slowly. She explained that Sammy had something called dyslexia. "This doesn't mean that he is sick or that he is not intelligent," she said, "but that he has a different way of learning than most other students. It is something he is born with, and we must all be understanding and kind as he progresses through school."

Ego nodded and left the classroom. On his way to the cafeteria, he saw Sammy. As he neared, Ego gave him a thumbs up and said, "Good book report, Sammy!"

Sammy, who looked like he had been bracing himself for one of Ego's mean comments, gave a big sigh of relief, and a smile replaced the worried look on his face as he said, "Thanks!"

On Saturday, there was a meeting of the Youth Fun Festival Game committee. During discussions, Ego remained quiet but not bored nor defensive. He actually politely listened as Pastor Jay asked Nora to explain more about her dunking game idea. Ego realized that the game did sound like fun and that they probably would raise a lot of money for the Youth Trip by dunking Pastor Jay. Suddenly, Ego thought of something that might make the game even more fun. At the end of the meeting, he approached Pastor Jay and Nora with his idea.

Sunday afternoon, light-lavender-skinned Ego and his family arrived at the Youth Fun Festival. Ego mentioned to his father that he really needed to go share some news with the King of Children's Hearts. His dad told him to go right away. Ego found the King in the youth study hall. The King was so happy to see Ego and hear about his past few days.

He said, "Dear child, I know that this was a difficult problem to work on."

Ego agreed and went on to share how hard it was to not charge ahead and do things yourself instead of including others, like with his sister, and how quickly he always seemed to want to criticize first instead of finding out more about a person, like with his classmate Sammy.

He also said, "Dear King, thank you for helping me by sending me the message to be quiet, listen, and investigate later. When my teacher told me about what Sammy was born with, I sure felt bad about the mean things I've said about him in the past." The King nodded.

Ego continued, "It felt good to try to encourage instead of criticizing. The smiles on my sister's and on Sammy's faces made me feel good too. I also learned that it's a good plan to actually give others a chance to talk and share their ideas, without my being a know-it-all and talking over them or putting them down to make myself look better."

The King smiled and said, "Yes, Ego, humility is one of the healthiest qualities my children can have as everyone benefits. And one of the best signs of humility is being willing to learn—having a heart that is teachable."

Ego looked at the clock on the wall, jumped up, and said, "In fact, Nora's idea about the dunking game really was a good one. But, dear King, I think I helped make it even better."

"How?" the King asked.

"By joining Pastor Jay as one of the people getting dunked! I imagine there are a lot of people who would like to give me a dunkin', and I deserve it!" he said.

The King chuckled as Ego raced off to get into his swimming trunks, his pink face flushed with excitement.

Study Questions:

1. Was it right for Ego to call people dumb or stupid?
2. Did the King think that pride would be easy to fix?
3. Where did Ego meet the King and where can you meet him?

Thinkin' Cap Questions:

1. Which is easier, criticizing or helping others?
2. Do you have a teachable heart?

Find the mystery character word.

About the Author

Barbara Bricker enjoys her faith, friends and family—especially her grandchildren—reading, and living in the Blue Ridge Mountains. She hopes her first literary effort helps children identify sinful feelings, learn how to work on those feelings, and draw closer to the King as they do so. The author would like to say a special thank you to Caleb for his listening ear.

Printed in the USA
CPSIA information can be obtained
at www.ICGtesting.com
LVHW061745260324
775529LV00015B/182